Flame of the Uncharted Heart

essential poetry

Other books from
California Health Publications

Touching the Mountain — The Self-Breema Handbook: Ancient
Exercises for the Modern World

Walking Into the Sun: Stories My Grandfather Told

Flame of the Uncharted Heart

essential poetry

Collected by Jon Schreiber

Illustrated by Celeste McLean

Published by
California Health Publications
Oakland, California

Address all inquiries to:

California Health Publications
6201 Florio Street, Suite 1A
Oakland, CA 94618

(510) 428-1283

ISBN: 0-9623581-4-2

Library of Congress Catalog Card Number: 92-73319

Printed in the United States of America

Text printed on recycled paper.

To all those who have desire for Understanding
and Presence in the heart

Contents

How This Book Came About

Once in a great while, Manocher Movlai would delight his students at the Institute for Health Improvement by spontaneously reciting an ancient poem of Rumi, Attar, Firdowsi, or of another Persian or Sufi poet, and translating it. I had been pestering him unsuccessfully for years to do a book of their poems (many have never been translated). My efforts to persuade him, by "coincidentally" reading a book of Rumi's poetry whenever we happened to meet, finally paid off—although not quite in the form I expected.

Once he agreed, we met every day, after our early morning meetings about the daily affairs of the Institute. As we paced up and down the room, Manocher would recite a poem from memory while I wrote it down, scribbling furiously. I started working on the book, believing the poems to be, as Manocher told me, of ancient Persian origin and never before written either in their original Farsi nor in any other language—poems passed down orally through an unbroken lineage of poets. It later became apparent that Manocher was the author of these poems, and, in fact, was generating them spontaneously as we walked. Yet he refused any credit for them, saying he was only a conduit for the expression of material which has always existed: "How much credit can a jar take for the honey it holds? Or a riverbed for the water? Or a window for the sunlight passing through it?"

I have revised these poems as little as possible and only to make them more accessible to readers unfamiliar with Manocher's exceptionally original usage of the English language. My goal has been to catch these birds by the tail as they flew by, and let you have a glimpse of their particular beauty—all of which derives from the sacredness and majesty of everyday life.

—Jon Schreiber, Oakland, 1992

Jon Schreiber

Jon Schreiber is director of the Institute for Health Improvement and of Advanced Arts Breema Chiropractic in Oakland, California. Dr. Schreiber prepared for a traditional medical degree at Columbia University in New York and subsequently became interested in alternative approaches to health and healing. Concurrent with receiving his chiropractic degree from Palmer College of Chiropractic–West, he was introduced to Manocher Movlai and Breema bodywork. Finding the Breema method unique in its ability to vitalize and heal the body, Dr. Schreiber has devoted many years to studying and teaching this system. Besides caring for patients in his clinic, he maintains an active teaching schedule both nationally and internationally.

He has also devoted great energy to documenting various aspects of this unwritten tradition. His first book, *Touching the Mountain*, is an illustrated guide for doing Self-Breema exercises. *Walking Into the Sun*, his second book, is a collection of stories told by Manocher Movlai that, like *Flame of the Uncharted Heart*, presents inspirational yet practical wisdom from the poetic side of this tradition. He is currently at work on a book documenting and explaining the effectiveness of the Breema method in addressing modern health concerns.

Man and God

Many of the poems use male pronouns in reference to animals, objects, and God. This usage reflects Manocher Movlai's Persian and Kurdish linguistic and cultural background, and my desire to present each poem in a version as close to the original as possible. I encourage you to expand the meaning of these male pronouns to include both female and male, as this is clearly the author's intent. The philosophy and principles which underlie the poems emphasize the unification of energy. Yin and yang, female and male, are simply two manifestations of the one life energy.

It's difficult for most people to hear the word 'God' without all kinds of associations, many of which come from their early religious training. When I expressed my concerns that readers might be put off by the frequent references to God in these poems, Manocher told me, "That's good! We are breaking their crystallizations about God. I'm not talking about the God somewhere up there, holding a weapon in his hand, waiting to reward our good behavior or punish us for our misdeeds. That's the God that doesn't fit into this poetry. I'm talking about God who is the fragrance of a ripe apricot."

Reading the Poems

Manocher asked me to pass along a few of his suggestions for enjoying the poems.

First, read one to yourself a few times, to become familiar with it. Then read it out loud. Listen not only to the words, but to the sounds they make. Listen to the words and their sequence "the way you would listen to an ocean wave as it breaks on the shore—or to rain hitting the roof on a quiet night—or to cold spring water being poured into a glass when you're hot and thirsty."

What about the poem's meaning? "Don't try to grasp the meaning. Allow the meaning to grasp you."

Acknowledgements

Two of Manocher's most beautiful poems, one dictated on October 19, 1991, and the other on October 20, were lost forever when my house burned down in the great Oakland Firestorm. The second poem had existed in written form for only an hour before it went up in flames. When I asked Manocher to repeat them the morning after the fire, he smiled and said, "Those poems weren't for this planet, Jon!"

I'd like to thank the following people for their help and support in making this book:

Manocher Movlai, Susan Varner, Gretchen Brandt, Cathy Vahsen, Carlene Schnabel, Denise Berezonsky, Celeste McLean, Ann Hudson, Ashik Staud, Marian Clark, Mary Cuneo, Dana Zed, Eliane Walis, Rona Spalten, Robin Somerville, Pari Schneider, Roxanne Schroter, Peter Hensel, Brenda Beebe, Jon Lobdell, Larry Stefl, Sharyn Venit, Don Cohen, Karen Bilgrai, Shannon Schroter, Heather Osterman, Armen Havanassian, Richard Grossinger, Lida Abramian, Joe Quackenbush, William and Frances Schreiber, Rachel and Jeremy Evnine, Matt Schreiber, Moira Little, Gail Riley, Sharon, Andrew, Steven, and Jennifer Resler, Christie Ahlf, Beth Kellman, Peter Lisker, Jose Ruiz, Mary Ann Finch, Rafael, Maya Danino, the Schertzer family, Regan Bice, William Jackson, Witter Bynner, Coleman Barks, Jan David Winitz, Michael Irwin, Christine Hunt, Aron Saltiel, Nancy Crum, Mary Green, Caite Bennett, Jon Brandt, Lisa Sternlieb, Rob Valentine, Karen Meyer, Nahman Kleinberg, David Curry, Steve Long, Jean Haseltine, Sayre Van Young, Irene Newmark, Janet Chann, Tatjana Kopp, Janet Madden.

Flame of the Uncharted Heart

essential poetry

My heart has many songs.
Sometimes
my soul is thirsty to hear them.
Oh, Friend, come enjoy the spring.
The overflowing water purifies itself.

A CHILDREN'S POEM

Mountain looked at his watch
and said,
"Oh Lord! It's late,
and Sun will shine any minute.
    Help me
        to be alive
and have the proper posture
toward my dear Giving Friend."

An eagle flying by
heard the mountain's prayer
and landed.

"My dear teacher," he began.
"We always receive our daily bread.
Look at the wild tulips.
The sun has filled them up with Life.
Now *they've* opened,
offering the resin of the Sun
to the honey bees,
who don't mind if the little birds enjoy
 a taste of heaven themselves."

Any stone
regardless of its shape and quality
makes an eternal ripple
when dropped into the ocean of Existence.

Oh, Lord of the Fire!
Allow me to be burned
with the flame of the heart
So may I quench my eternal thirst
in the no-things.

One spring morning, before sunrise
When the song of the birds filled the garden
And the branches of the peach tree were in
    full blossom,
I saw myself—
Wonderstruck with nature.
And I heard the deep sound
    in my soul
I am alive.

Sparrows
sit on a branch
of the silver tree
taking a sunbath.
Peeping every now and then
searching under their wings.
Their sounds please the ear
and touch the heart.
Oh, Lord of Life!
Many thanks for the gift
of Life!
Many thanks for the ability
to feel gratitude.

How large the ocean seems to a drop
and how small is that drop in the ocean.
When the bond is
love to exist
Where is the measurement?
Isn't Existence
but a point,
but a moment?
When love touches the core
of the being,
everything becomes nothing
and nothing becomes everything.
Oh, Lord of Light!
Allow me to be a particle of Light
penetrating all that is.

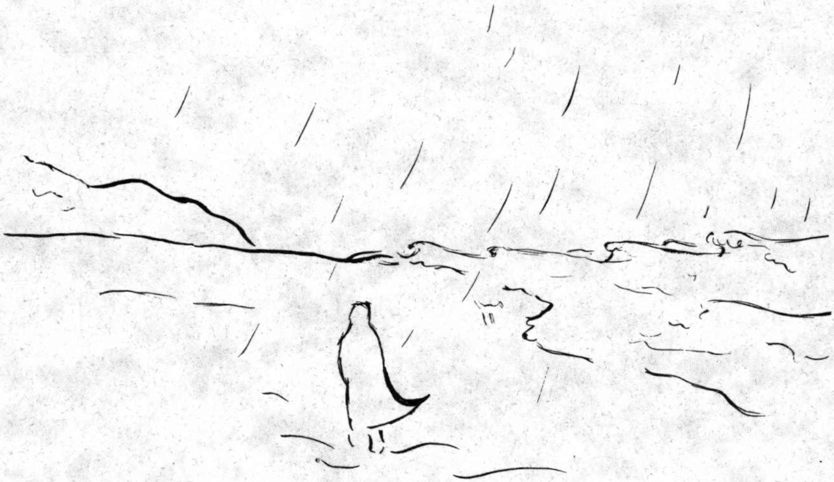

In the early morning summerday
    it was cool yet.
Sitting on a stone,
    close enough to hear
the humming hives of the honey bees
    on one side,
the music of the flowing spring
    on the other.
They brought me to the majestic moment
    of silence.

Oh, dear Existence!
Allow all that exists
    to be filled
    with love for Life!
From the everlasting flow of light,
    give them peace
    in their hearts.

I wish to be the stone
that's tossed into the pond.
I wish to be the sound
that goes *"pa'loup"*
when the stone hits the water.
I wish to be the water
that receives the stone and the sound.
I wish to be the silence
that is beyond all happenings.

When I think of you
the sun shines
in my midnight.
And in mid-day
I experience
the cool and living silence
of the night.

Since the love for you
made me free
from day and night
I also
do not know
beginning and end.
So my mind feels
that which is all
and my heart thinks
that which is no-thing.

Oh, Lord of the Moment!
Shine the light of the Timeless
to the Spaceless
universe.

When, through Awareness,
the life in air,
water, fire, earth, and ether
is seen and felt,
these forms are transformed
into formless Existence.

Oh, Lord of Light!
You see the movement inside a stone
and the changing textures of silence.
Who drinks the elixir of Life,
in a moment of heartfelt joy
sees one flame,
        ever shining,
        everlasting.

When the shepherd's nai
echoes on the mountain,
the sheep's appetite
for grazing grass and herbs and greeneries
increases.

In gratitude
they swallow the air with their noses
and the music with their ears.
In their eyes you can see
a friendly look at all that surrounds them.

Then there's a moment of rest—
the shepherd's taking his afternoon nap
and the sheep gather
close to him
still hearing the sound of his flute
in the running creek
that passes between the rows of trees
and penetrates the field.

Oh, Lord of Light!
Be my shepherd
and allow me to hear
the sound of your Existence.
Let me exist in you
and you in me.

A couple of leaves
floating swiftly
     on the surface of the creek
spoke as they passed:
Where are you going, if I may ask?
To the ocean, dear friend.

I wish I could have asked
where they come from
but it was too late.
At least I know where they're going.

And then I said,
If that's where everything goes,
maybe that's where it all comes from, too.

Oh, Lord of the Ocean!
Allow me to be an ever-knowing drop
in the Beginningless
Endless
Ocean of Existence,
giving rise
to endless waves
     of thought
          and feeling
in the depth of my eternal silence.

Early morning,
just before sunrise.
A few twigs in the flame.
Teapot steaming,
and the wine-red tea
in the teacups.

The old man says,
*I wonder what God's having
for breakfast this morning?*

Then he answers himself:
*Probably a cup of tea
and fresh-baked bread.
One has taste,
and the other, the aroma
of Existence.*

A tall, gorgeous mountain stands
amid its relatives of varying height,
not thinking of itself.
Appreciating the sound and the movement
of the running river.
Along the riverbank,
wildflowers form a tablecloth
of textures, colors, and aromas
celebrating life.

Here comes night;
stars appear in the sky,
creating arrangements of utmost beauty—
magnificent formations of light.
The ears of the silence listen
to the sounds of the sky.

Stars,
river,
flowers,
and the mountain
remind us
of the blessing of Existence
in every moment.
Oh, Lord of Light!
Let me partake
in this majestic feast
of silence.

A few sparrows in the field
were taking a dust bath.

One of them said:
How great it feels—
the warmth of the sun
on this soil.
I wonder
if this soil enjoys
Life in this moment
as much as I do?

Another said:
How do you know
this joy you experience
isn't the same joy
that soil received from the sun,
and is now handing down to you?

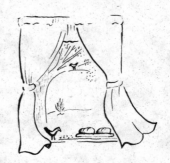

The third said:
Oh!
If this joy you're talking about
is real joy,
it has to come from within.
What has it got to do with
the soil and the sun?
Or with you, little sister?

The fourth one said:
Brother, you philosopher!
You always create division.

First between you and the soil,
then between the soil and sun,
now between inner and outer.
If there is joy,
it is
all that is.
How could joy be a property of the inner,
but not the outer?
That means joy with opposition.
It has far to go
to become joy
in the real sense.
Not separate
from you, soil, sun, and
everything that is.
The God of Love manifests in vibration,
and there is only one wave, everlasting,
which contains all that exists.

The fifth sparrow:
So much talk!
I'm flying to the neighbors' field.
It's after lunch,
and I can almost taste the sweet aroma
of the crumbs that fell
from their fresh baked bread.

Between nothingness
and all things
there is a consciousness.
The flame of that consciousness
is Awareness.
And the light that shines through that Awareness
is God.

As River flows
the banks are nurtured.
River didn't name the banks
nor dictate their experience.

Opposites are created
when we forget
the reality
of the everflowing
      everlasting
      beginningless
      endless
water of life.

Oh, Lord of the Water!
Give me purpose!
Fulfill all who have desire
to grow
so the Light of the Sky
can look upon Existence
with a smile.

In the field of Existence
where God is

        sunlight

      water

  air

    soil

      and ether,

everything
has the possibility to grow
eternally.
Oh, Light of the Eternal Everlasting!
Allow me to love life
in each
    and every moment.
Let me be
a perfect gardener
in the garden of all possibilities.

Children playing in the field
run, yell, and laugh,
hiding behind the trees.
They're smelling flowers,
touching grass,
dangling their feet in the creek.
Splashing water,
they laugh some more.

Behind the window,
standing, watching, listening,
I wait.

Oh, Dearest of All!
Allow me to be
like the little kids—
Pure.
Uncalculating.
Delighting in all that is.

When a sun ray hits the mirror,

it reflects

and creates more light.

Every cell and particle

in Existence

also reflects

light and life.

In the unity of all things

sprouts the genuine

seed of love.

Love that

has no object

has no subject

is only substance—

and so

is precious

to the Heart

of Man.

There is so much
    to hear
There is so much
    to read
There is so much
    to know
and to realize.

Oh, Lord of all Knowing
    and Un-knowing!
Help me
to have Being-Knowledge
So I can fulfill
and be fulfilled
by your presence.

Life is...

throwing a stone in the pond

sound

smile

silence

eternal,

Beginningless and Endless

come together.

New Life.

God.

Existence in the Being of all things.

Nurture the desire for growth!
That's the law Nature follows.
But the desire has to be there,
ready to take form.
When the form accords
with Nature's gift,
harmony is created—
harmony that holds
the revitalizing force of Nature.

And so Nature supports itself
by nourishing everything it touches.
Every cell in the body is nourished
by Nature,
and by nature
provides nourishment.
That's the way
cells create
unity
from diversity.

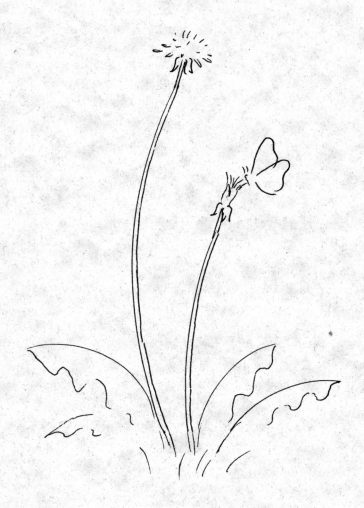

God is the materiality
of everything that exists.
Awareness of this materiality
is God's consciousness.
Awakening of this consciousness
gives Love of Existence.

Oh, Lord of Light—
Allow me to be in Love
    with everything that exists.

I am alive.
I walk in the street—
jugglers are tossing their balls to the sky
and catching them again.
Many many balls.
The clown with a sympathetic face
and funny nose
smiles and wiggles his tails.
Some children laugh.
Children, clown, jugglers, crowd,
and myself,
alive.

Passing through the crowded streets—
shopkeepers chat amiably with customers.
A few exchanges,
a few things are traded.
Some are still looking.
Shopkeepers, street, buyers, lookers, things,
and myself,
alive.

Entering the coffee shop—
ordering coffee,
seeing the lines.
Some buy from the deli-bars.
Some get a pot of tea,
order of cappucino,
cafe-latte,
some cookies, some delights,
some middle-eastern foods.

The sound of the dishes,
of the chairs moving around,
of the conversations,
the faces of people,
and myself,
alive.

Back to the street—
looking at the trees.
Robins are searching
branch by branch.
A few sparrows.
Sunlight on the branches,
some shade on the ground,
smile on my face.
Smile, and me, and everything that is,
alive.

You reading this poem,
you walking to those places,
you hearing the noise,
you tasting the coffee,
you and I,
and this poem,
alive.

Creation
is God's cosmic poetry.
Take this poetry
into your heart, and
Beyond time and space—
you are.

When the cherry tree is filled with blossoms
it gives visual pleasure—
that's information.
When the blossoms become cherries
and ripen—
that's knowledge.
When the cherries are eaten
and nurture every cell—
that is understanding.

My ears and eyes
collect the blossoms.
My contemplation and meditation
turn the blossoms to cherries.
My ability to receive—
this is actual eating.

Oh, Lord of Life!
Allow my trees to be healthy
in the roots.
Fill them with blossoms
and fruit.
Let the fruit ripen
and nurture all life.

In the center
of the field of Light
there is a light.
And in its center
another light.
Where the center
and the field
form a single point,
the majestic Kingdom of God exists.
At one
with all creation.
At peace
with manifested and un-manifested.

Look from there at creation;
blessings and joy fill the heart.
Think of that which is;
the light of Awareness fills the mind.
Love creation;
there is boundless belonging.

Oh, Lord of Light!
Allow us to inhale and exhale
the blessing of this Existence.

When Day and Night meet
When Time and Timeless meet
When Space and Spaceless meet
When God and Man meet
When You and I meet
There is recognition
of the unity
of all things.

Oh, Lord of all Light!
Grant me a moment
of Existence,
to be
and recognize
that
I am.

Ocean is nothing
but a drop
in the moment.
Drop is ocean
in Eternity.
In the timeless and spaceless,
there is manifested
and un-manifested
Existence.
In the gap
between manifested
and un-manifested;
Silence
Reality
Love of God
Truth
A Moment.

In the quiet of the morning,
running creek sang a song,
conversing with the birds
on the tall palm trees.
Looking at the mountain
in its majesty,
listening to the conversation,
fresh air entering my lungs.
In the meadow of my existence,
many flowers were opening.
Each had an attribute
and fragrance
of the love for life.

God and nature
looking at each other
peacefully,
as if one,
admiring all that exists.
One short moment,
but eternal,
the instrument of harmony
was playing a song
in the forest.

Oh, Lord of Light!
Allow us to participate
in our life
always and everywhere.

In the quiet of the morning,
in the noise of mid-day,
in the mystical character of the night,
there is a heartbeat,
in harmony with the pendulum of existence,
swinging to the yes
        and no.

And right there,
in the very gap
between the two,
an infinite possibility
to know God.

In the heart of each moment
there is the seed
of all potential.
When you and I enter the moment,
Existence smiles.

Oh, Lord of the Clouds!
Let the white raindrops nurture
all that is.
May those who have desire to grow
do so
by giving service
to all life.

When the energy of life
passes through me,
it speaks of God.
When the energy of me
passes through life,
it speaks of man.
In fact, there is no me
or life
or energy
or speaking
or passing through—
There is only God.

Wildflowers receive the morning breeze,
dancing to the song of the running creek.
The rocks, skins smooth
from the time they spent underwater,
are a very peaceful audience.
The mountain energizes all activity
with the first ray of light from its peak
waking the birds.
Their sound quickly grows
into a majestic chanting.

Everything celebrates with joy
the observer
who, by registering,
comes closer
to Being Life.

Sound and silence
are two qualities
of the one moment.
Being present in the moment
is the highest gift Existence bestows.

I love friendship.
It's wonderful that
my friends are growing.
Just this morning
the jacaranda tree smiled warmly at me.
But that wasn't all,
because when I listened
the birds were greeting me
with harmony and joy.

The big rock
sitting by itself
was so happy to see me,
I felt any moment
its arms would open wide
for a morning hug.
The running water assured me;
our deep relationship would continue
on the best of terms.

Friends
with that much affection
don't give God a chance
for anything
but to smile at Existence.

What is sound?
Essence of silence.
And yet silence
is the foundation of sound.
Existence is exalted
by manifestation,
yet the un-manifested is named
as its warp and weft.

These are just words—
but behind the words,
an un-verbal moment
Where you and I
and God
know each other.
Then again we separate,
and by the magnetic force of attraction
we resume the search.

The world of
what
where
how
when
why
is outside the circumference.
On the circumference—
dancing phenomena.
In the circle—
Life.
In the center—
Moment.

In the heart of the night—
the smile of the morning.
In the morning's progress—
the depth of night.
In the wondering cell—
the clarity of all Existence.
Yet clarity is pregnant
with its own opposition.
In the pendulum of time and space—
Timeless and Spaceless.

Once the heart of the lily
transforms your soul,
you'll see God in everything.

Into the darkness
of confusion,
bring the candlelight
of fact.
Desire the sunlight
of clear knowing—
you may enter
the flame
of the uncharted heart.

Other titles by Jon Schreiber, available from California Health Publications:

Touching the Mountain—
The Self-Breema Handbook:
Ancient Exercises for the Modern World

For centuries, the mountain villagers of Breemava have practiced a simple series of exercises to create vibrant health, vitality, and inner harmony. Based on the highest laws of nature, Self-Breema exercises activate the body's self-healing forces. Now, for the first time, these treasured secrets are available to Western readers.

This easy-to-follow manual will initiate you into the extraordinary world of Self-Breema, introduce you to the many benefits of this powerful system, and show you how, in just minutes a day, you can transform tension, stress, and fatigue into new energy and vitality.

"An effective guide for enhancing a person's mental, physical, and spiritual health. A unique fusion of Western physiology and Oriental philosophy...a most insightful book."

—Dr. Kenneth Pelletier, author of
Mind as Healer, Mind as Slayer

Walking Into the Sun:
Stories My Grandfather Told

Here's a collection of delightful tales and wise sayings recounted by a master storyteller from a remote village high in the Kurdish mountains. Drawn from Kurdish, Persian, Afghani, and Sufi traditions, and from his own extraordinary experiences, most have never before appeared in print.

These stories take you on adventures with kings and shepherds, magicians and millionaires, thieves and holy men. You'll travel across cultures and through the ages—from Tabriz to Times Square, from the days of King Solomon to the present—by train, sports car, and donkey.

Charming and unconventional, each story is an exuberant celebration of the depth and mystery of life. Passed from generation to generation, these tales have reached us without losing the purity of their original message. As the storyteller himself says:

> "Truth has a ring to it.
> You hear it, you wake up."

ORDER FORM

Please send me:

_____ copies of **Touching the Mountain—The Self-Breema Handbook**
$24.95 + $2.30 per order* for shipping
California residents add $2.06 sales tax per book

_____ copies of **Walking Into the Sun: Stories My Grandfather Told**
$9.95 + $2.30 per order* for shipping
California residents add 82¢ sales tax per book

_____ copies of **Flame of the Uncharted Heart: Essential Poetry**
$14.95 + $2.30 per order* for shipping
California residents add $1.23 sales tax per book

* You may combine orders of any book and pay just $2.30 per order for shipping.

Enclosed is my check or money order for $_____,
payable to:

California Health Publications
6201 Florio Street
Oakland, CA 94618

Name_____

Address_____

City_____State_____Zip_____

ORDER FORM

Please send me:

_____ copies of **Touching the Mountain—The Self-Breema Handbook**
$24.95 + $2.30 per order* for shipping
California residents add $2.06 sales tax per book

_____ copies of **Walking Into the Sun: Stories My Grandfather Told**
$9.95 + $2.30 per order* for shipping
California residents add 82¢ sales tax per book

_____ copies of **Flame of the Uncharted Heart: Essential Poetry**
$14.95 + $2.30 per order* for shipping
California residents add $1.23 sales tax per book

* You may combine orders of any book and pay just $2.30 per order for shipping.

Enclosed is my check or money order for $_____,
payable to:

California Health Publications
6201 Florio Street
Oakland, CA 94618

Name_____

Address_____

City_____State_____Zip_____